D0848349

# Magical History Tour

## THE SAMURAI

**FABRICE ERRE**
Writer

**SYLVAIN SAVOIA**
Artist

MIAMI

# Magical History Tour

## #12 "The Samurai"

By Fabrice Erre and Sylvain Savoia

Original series editors: Frédéric Niffle and Lewis Trondheim
Colors: Sylvain Savoia
Colors Assistant: Luc Perdriset
Translation: Nanette McGuinness

Mark McNabb – Production
Wilson Ramos Jr. – Letterer
Zachary Harris — Editorial Intern
Stephanie Brooks — Assistant Editor
Rex Ogle — Editorial Director
Jim Salicrup
Editor-in-Chief

Papercutz was founded by Terry Nantier and Jim Salicrup.

ISBN 978-1-5458-1034-7

Printed in China
April 2023

First Papercutz Printing

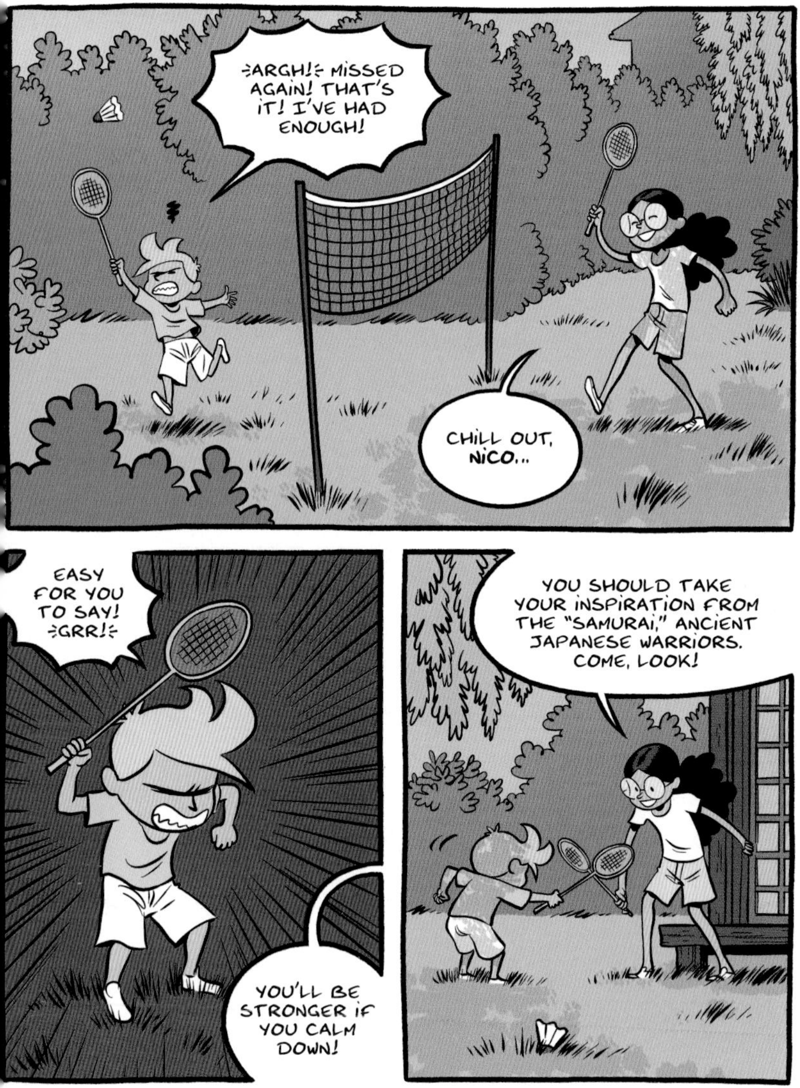

ARGH! MISSED AGAIN! THAT'S IT! I'VE HAD ENOUGH!
CHILL OUT, NICO...
EASY FOR YOU TO SAY! GRR!
YOU'LL BE STRONGER IF YOU CALM DOWN!
YOU SHOULD TAKE YOUR INSPIRATION FROM THE "SAMURAI," ANCIENT JAPANESE WARRIORS. COME, LOOK!

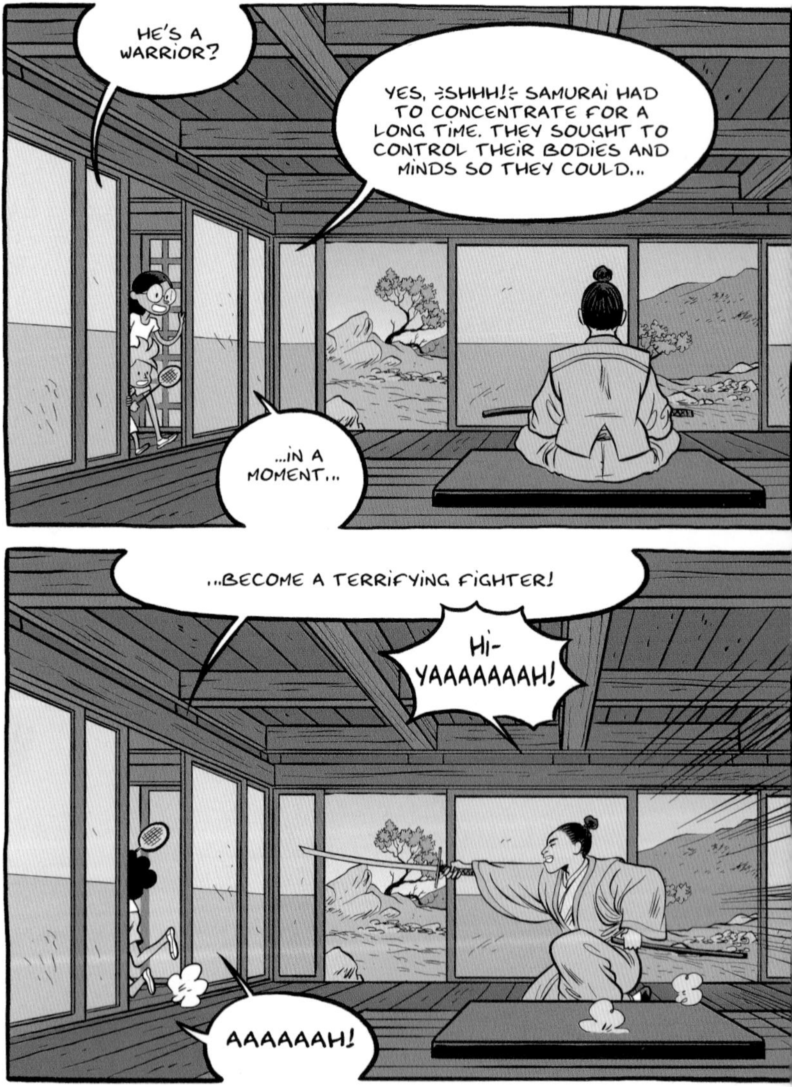
HE'S A WARRIOR?
YES, =SHHH!= SAMURAI HAD TO CONCENTRATE FOR A LONG TIME. THEY SOUGHT TO CONTROL THEIR BODIES AND MINDS SO THEY COULD...
...IN A MOMENT...
...BECOME A TERRIFYING FIGHTER!
HI-YAAAAAAAH!
AAAAAAH!

SAMURAI ARE VERY IMPORTANT IN THE HISTORY OF JAPAN.

ARE THEY THE ONES WHO FOUNDED IT?

ACCORDING TO JAPANESE LEGENDS, EMPEROR JIMMU WAS A DESCENDANT OF A GODDESS AND FOUNDED THE COUNTRY IN THE 7TH CENTURY B.C.E.

BUT THE EMPERORS' POWER WAS CHALLENGED IN THE 12TH CENTURY C.E. THAT'S WHEN THE AGE OF THE SAMURAI BEGAN. IT LASTED 700 YEARS!

ORIGINALLY, SAMURAI WERE SOLDIERS IN A LORD'S SERVICE: THEIR NAME MEANS "HE WHO SERVES."

THEY FIRST WERE PEASANTS WHO TOOK UP ARMS WHEN THEIR LORD NEEDED THEM. THEN IT BECAME A JOB.

JAPANESE LORDS WAGED WAR AGAINST EACH OTHER?

YES, TWO LARGE CLANS FOUGHT EACH OTHER FROM 1180-1185 IN THE GENPEI WAR.

平氏

源氏

IN 1192, THE VICTOR, MINAMOTO NO YORITOMO, BECAME THE "SHOGUN," WHICH MEANS THE "GREAT GENERAL, SUBJUGATOR OF BARBARIANS."

HE TOOK POWER AND MADE THE EMPEROR STAY IN HIS PALACE.

6

THE SHOGUN SET UP A "BAKUFU," A MILITARY GOVERNMENT THAT RULED JAPAN FROM THEN ON.

THERE WAS A PYRAMID OF POWER. SAMURAI BECAME VERY IMPORTANT.

EMPEROR: A SYMBOLIC, RELIGIOUS ROLE.

SHOGUN: THE TRUE POLITICAL AND MILITARY LEADER OF JAPAN.

DAIMYOS: THE GREAT LORDS.

SAMURAI: MAINTAINED ORDER.

THE REST OF THE POPULATION: PEASANTS, ARTISANS...

THE PEOPLE FEARED AND RESPECTED SAMURAI.

LOWER YOUR HEAD. HE COULD CUT IT OFF!

HUH?

THEY HAD A VERY... STRONG SENSE OF HONOR.

THEY WERE THE ONLY ONES ALLOWED TO CARRY WEAPONS. THEY COULDN'T HOLD A JOB SUCH AS PEASANT OR MERCHANT.

HEY! BEING A SAMURAI SOUNDS GREAT!

YOU'RE FORGETTING THEY HAD TO FIGHT AND BE READY TO GIVE THEIR LIVES FOR THEIR MASTERS... THAT WAS THEIR JOB.

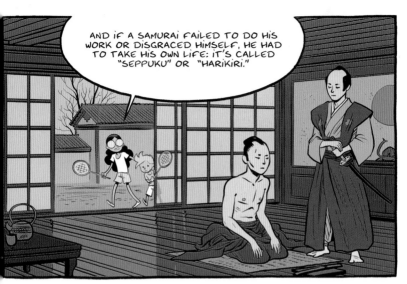

AND IF A SAMURAI FAILED TO DO HIS WORK OR DISGRACED HIMSELF, HE HAD TO TAKE HIS OWN LIFE: IT'S CALLED "SEPPUKU" OR "HARIKIRI."

HE HAD TO SLICE OPEN HIS ABDOMEN AND THEN ANOTHER SAMURAI BEHEADED HIM.

≑GULP!≑

EVEN THEN, THEY HAD TO STAY CALM.

I HAVE NEITHER LIFE NOR DEATH. I MAKE THE ETERNAL MY LIFE AND MY DEATH.

LET'S NOT STAY HERE...

TO GET TO BE SO STRONG, SAMURAI WERE TRAINED FROM CHILDHOOD. THEY WERE GENERALLY SONS OF FIGHTERS.

THEY WERE TAUGHT NOT TO SHOW THEIR FEELINGS FROM THE TIME THEY WERE VERY YOUNG...

NOT TO GRIPE WHEN THEY MISS THE SHUTTLECOCK IN BADMINTON, FOR EXAMPLE.

THEY PRACTICED USING WEAPONS IN SPECIAL SCHOOLS CALLED "KORYU."

WE LEARN MATH AND THEY LEARNED WEAPONS?!

YES, THAT DISCIPLINE'S CALLED "KENJUTSU." BUT THEY ALSO LEARNED SELF-CONTROL AND HOW TO CONCENTRATE.

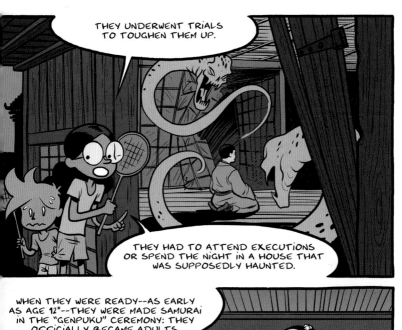

THEY UNDERWENT TRIALS TO TOUGHEN THEM UP.

THEY HAD TO ATTEND EXECUTIONS OR SPEND THE NIGHT IN A HOUSE THAT WAS SUPPOSEDLY HAUNTED.

WHEN THEY WERE READY--AS EARLY AS AGE 12*--THEY WERE MADE SAMURAI IN THE "GENPUKU" CEREMONY; THEY OFFICIALLY BECAME ADULTS.

THEN THEY CHANGED THEIR HAIRSTYLE AND NAME AND GOT THEIR WEAPON.

*THE AGE RANGE WAS 12-18 AND THE AVERAGE AGE FOR THE GENPUKU CEREMONY WAS 15.

SO, WHAT ABOUT GIRLS?

AH, THEY COULD NEVER BECOME SAMURAI.

THERE WERE WOMEN WARRIORS, CALLED "ONNA-MUSHA."

ARCHEOLOGISTS, HOWEVER, HAVE FOUND SOME BATTLE SITES THAT HAVE MANY FEMALE SKELETONS.

TOMOE GOZEN, FOR EXAMPLE, WOULD HAVE FOUGHT IN THE GENPEI WAR AND EVEN COMMANDED TROOPS, BUT WE KNOW VERY LITTLE ABOUT HER...

MORE GENERALLY, WOMEN WERE KEPT OUT OF THINGS. NOBLEMEN'S WIVES WERE CALLED "OKUGATA-SAMA."

THAT BEING SAID, SAMURAI'S WIVES HAD TO BE ABLE TO DEFEND THEIR HOMES WHEN THEIR HUSBANDS WERE GONE.

THEY USED SWORDS?

SOMETIMES, BUT PARTICULARLY THE "NAGINATA," SORT OF A LANCE WITH A BLADE.

THEY ALSO HAD TO DEFEND THEIR HONOR IF ALL WAS LOST AND KILL THEMSELVES.

BY SLICING OPEN THEIR STOMACHS?

NO, THEIR THROATS.

SO, THE SWORD REALLY WAS THE WEAPON RESERVED FOR SAMURAI?

YES, BUT THEY USED OTHER WEAPONS, TOO!

ACTUALLY, THE FIRST SAMURAI WERE HORSE ARCHERS.

THEY COULD BE VERY PRECISE WHILE GALLOPING!

THE "KATANA," A LONG SWORD, BECAME THEIR MAIN WEAPON IN THE 14TH CENTURY.

THEY WERE VERY COMPLICATED TO MAKE. MOST WERE FORGED IN THE VILLAGE OF SEKI, WHERE THE BLACKSMITHS' SECRETS WERE WELL-KEPT.

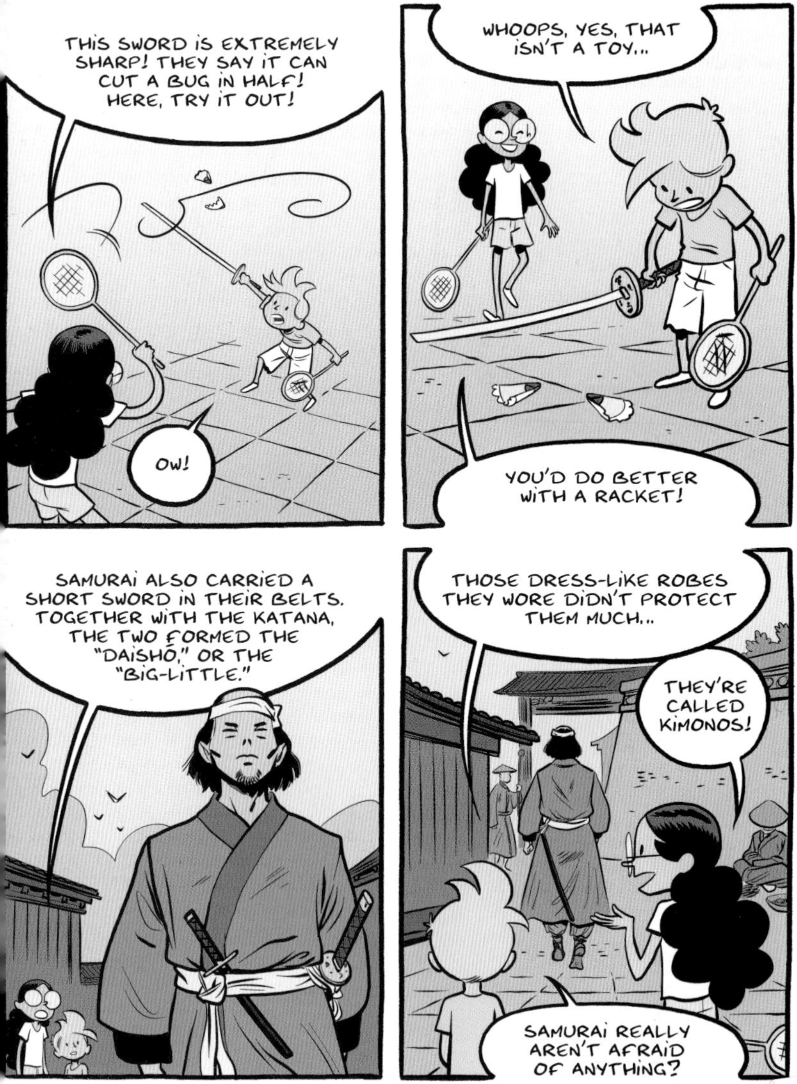
THIS SWORD IS EXTREMELY SHARP! THEY SAY IT CAN CUT A BUG IN HALF! HERE, TRY IT OUT!
OW!
WHOOPS, YES, THAT ISN'T A TOY...
YOU'D DO BETTER WITH A RACKET!
SAMURAI ALSO CARRIED A SHORT SWORD IN THEIR BELTS. TOGETHER WITH THE KATANA, THE TWO FORMED THE "DAISHŌ," OR THE "BIG-LITTLE."
THOSE DRESS-LIKE ROBES THEY WORE DIDN'T PROTECT THEM MUCH...
THEY'RE CALLED KIMONOS!
SAMURAI REALLY AREN'T AFRAID OF ANYTHING?

THE SAMURAI'S IDEAL WAS A DUEL--A FIGHT WITH PRECISE RULES AND RESPECT FOR EACH PERSON'S HONOR.

THEY GREETED EACH OTHER AND EXCHANGED NAMES BEFORE STARTING. THEY EVEN COMPLIMENTED THE LOSER BEFORE BEHEADING HIM.

LIKE IN BADMINTON... EXCEPT THE BIT ABOUT BEHEADING, OF COURSE.

IN THESE SITUATIONS, THEY COULD FIGHT FAIR AND SQUARE, IN KIMONOS.

BUT IN WAR, BATTLES ARE MORE VIOLENT AND CONFUSED.

AAAAH!

SO, THEY PROTECTED THEMSELVES WITH ARMOR MADE OF IRON PLATES CONNECTED WITH SILK THREAD.

16

IT WAS MUCH LIGHTER AND MORE MOBILE THAN THE ARMOR EUROPEAN KNIGHTS FROM THAT TIME WORE.

HOW DID THEY RECOGNIZE EACH OTHER?

LOOK! THEY WORE A BANNER ATTACHED TO THEIR BACKS, A "SASHIMONO."

THEIR HELMET, CALLED A "KABUTO," WHICH PROTECTED THE HEAD AND NECK, WAS DECORATED TO HELP RECOGNIZE A SAMURAI AND HIS CLAN.

THEIR MASK, OR "MENPO," PROTECTED THEM BUT ALSO CAUSED FEAR: IT SOMETIMES DEPICTED THE FACE OF A DEMON!

WERE THERE A LOT OF WARS?

OH, YES. THEY HAD TO PROTECT THE COUNTRY FROM FOREIGN INVADERS.

IN 1281, THE MONGOL EMPEROR KUBLAI KHAN HEADED TO JAPAN WITH 4400 SHIPS.

THE SAMURAI DEFENDED THEIR LAND AND KEPT THEM FROM DISEMBARKING.

THEN THE SHIPS WERE DESTROYED BY A TYPHOON. THE WINDS WERE CALLED, "KAMIKAZE," WHICH MEANS "DIVINE WIND."

DID THE JAPANESE HAVE A NAVY, TOO?

YES, THEY TRIED TO CONQUER KOREA IN 1592, BUT THEY DIDN'T SUCCEED.

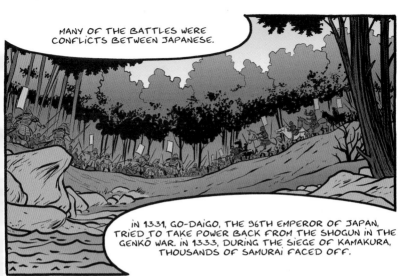

MANY OF THE BATTLES WERE CONFLICTS BETWEEN JAPANESE.

IN 1331, GO-DAIGO, THE 96TH EMPEROR OF JAPAN, TRIED TO TAKE POWER BACK FROM THE SHOGUN IN THE GENKŌ WAR. IN 1333, DURING THE SIEGE OF KAMAKURA, THOUSANDS OF SAMURAI FACED OFF.

≋ARGH!≋ THEY STILL CUT OFF THE HEADS OF THEIR ENEMIES!

YES, THE VICTORS BROUGHT THEM BACK TO THEIR DAIMYO TO PROVE THEIR WORTH.

EVENTUALLY A NEW SHOGUN WON THE WAR AND TOOK POWER... BUT THE SITUATION DETERIORATED IN THE NEXT CENTURY.

IN 1467, JAPAN ENTERED A DIFFICULT TIME, THE SENGOKU ("WARRING STATES") PERIOD--A CIVIL WAR THAT LASTED OVER 100 YEARS AND AFFECTED THE ENTIRE COUNTRY.

THE DAIMYOS FOUGHT EACH OTHER; THE SHOGUNS NO LONGER HAD POWER, NOR DID THE EMPEROR.

THEY BUILT STURDY CASTLES; THE FIRST FIREARMS ARRIVED IN JAPAN, BROUGHT BY THE EUROPEANS, WHICH CHANGED FIGHTING. MORE AND MORE SAMURAI WERE NEEDED TO DEAL WITH THIS.

IT WAS A TIME OF CONFUSION, THE LAW OF THE STRONGEST, AND NUMEROUS BETRAYALS. SOME SAMURAI CARVED OUT DOMAINS FOR THEMSELVES.

THE PERIOD ENDED IN 1600 WITH THE BATTLE OF SEKIGAHARA, THE BIGGEST IN THE HISTORY OF JAPAN. ALMOST 200,000 SAMURAI FACED EACH OTHER.

THAT'S TERRIBLE!

YES, BUT THAT SHOCK PUT AN END TO THIS TIME OF TURMOIL!

THE WINNER OF THE BATTLE, DAIMYO TOKUGAWA IEYASU, BECAME SHOGUN IN 1603. HE IMPOSED A PEACE THAT LASTED MORE THAN 250 YEARS, CALLED THE EDO PERIOD.

HE CONFISCATED THE FIREARMS AND DESTROYED THE CASTLES.

AH, THAT'S GOOD. YOU WERE TALKING ABOUT PEACE BUT THERE WASN'T MUCH OF THAT UP TO THEN!

YES, BUT MANY SAMURAI FOUND THEMSELVES UNEMPLOYED!

SINCE THEY'D HAD SOME EDUCATION, SOME BECAME TEACHERS; OTHERS BECAME ADMINISTRATORS WHO LEVIED TAXES...

BUT MOST ONLY KNEW HOW TO FIGHT.

IN ADDITION, SOME HAD LOST THEIR LORDS IN THE CIVIL WARS. THEY WERE CALLED "RŌNIN,"--"WAVE MEN," OR "VAGRANTS," BASICALLY ATTACHED TO NO ONE.

WHAT DID THEY DO TO SURVIVE?

THEY SERVED ANOTHER DAIMYO OR DEFENDED WHATEVER CAUSES THEY COULD FIND... BUT SOME BECAME BANDITS!

THAT ISN'T VERY "CHIVALROUS"!

NO, IT WASN'T! OTHER SAMURAI WHO WERE STILL HONORABLE FOUGHT THEM!

23

SINCE THEY WERE USELESS OR DANGEROUS, DID THE SAMURAI DISAPPEAR?

NOT AT ALL! THEY REMAINED VERY IMPORTANT IN JAPANESE SOCIETY, BUT THEIR ROLE CHANGED...

THE SAMURAI BECAME A KIND OF SYMBOL. THEY REPRESENTED AN IDEAL PERSON WITH QUALITIES TO TRY TO EMULATE.

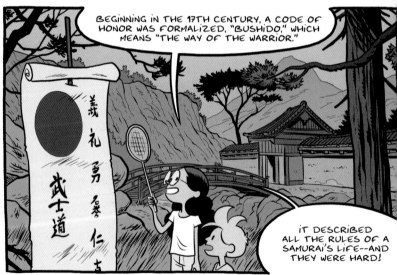

BEGINNING IN THE 17TH CENTURY, A CODE OF HONOR WAS FORMALIZED, "BUSHIDO," WHICH MEANS "THE WAY OF THE WARRIOR."

IT DESCRIBED ALL THE RULES OF A SAMURAI'S LIFE--AND THEY WERE HARD!

THE CODE EXPLAINED THE SEVEN ESSENTIAL QUALITIES OF THE SAMURAI!

勇 COURAGE

真 HONESTY

義 RECTITUDE

名誉 HONOR

仁 BENEVOLENCE

忠義 LOYALTY

礼 RESPECT

THAT'S WHY SAMURAI BEGAN DOING OTHER, MORE SPIRITUAL ACTIVITIES.

STILL, A WARRIOR IS A STRANGE ROLE MODEL IN A TIME OF PEACE.

SAMURAI DEVOTED MUCH OF THEIR TIME TO "ZEN."

DOES THAT MEAN, "SLEEPING"?

NO, IT MEANS "MEDITATION."

TO EMPTY THEIR MINDS, THEY DIDN'T MOVE, AND THEY FOCUSED ON THEIR BREATHING.

SAMURAI INVENTED THIS?

IT CAME FROM BUDDHIST MONKS, BUT SOME OF THEM CHANGED IT.

SUZUKI SHŌSAN, A SAMURAI WHO TOOK PART IN THE BATTLE OF SEKIGAHARA, LATER BECAME A MONK AND INFLUENCED MANY JAPANESE!

SAMURAI ALSO PRACTICED THE TEA CEREMONY, PREPARING THE DRINK WITH VERY SLOW MOVEMENTS THAT WERE ALWAYS THE SAME...

SEEKING PEACE WAS SUPPOSED TO LEAD THEM TOWARD THINKING PHILOSOPHICALLY, TO BEING WISE...

AH, THEN THEY DIDN'T BEHEAD ANYONE DURING THE CEREMONY?

THEY WEREN'T JUST BIG BRUTES! THEY DEVELOPED THEIR ARTISTRY, BELIEVE IT OR NOT...

CALLIGRAPHY, POETRY, DANCE...

THE COMPLETE SAMURAI OF THE EDO PERIOD FOLLOWED THE WAY OF THE PAINTBRUSH AND THE SWORD.

SOME "PERFECT" SAMURAI OF THIS TIME BECAME TRUE FIGURES OF LEGEND.

THIS IS MIYAMOTO MUSASHI, THE BEST-KNOWN SAMURAI! IMAGINE SIR LANCELOT AND MICHELANGELO IN THE SAME PERSON!

HE SURVIVED THE BATTLE OF SEKIGAHARA AND WON OVER 60 DUELS! YET IT WAS SAID HE FOUGHT WITH A WOODEN SWORD!

DURING HIS LIFE, HE ALSO CREATED MAGNIFICENT INK DRAWINGS AND WROTE SEVERAL BOOKS ON THE ART OF WAR.

28

THERE WERE ALSO GROUPS OF HEROIC SAMURAI.

IN 1701, A YOUNG DAIMYO WAS SENTENCED TO DEATH FOR WOUNDING A SHOGUN'S ASSISTANT. HIS SAMURAI CAME TOGETHER AS RONIN.

47 OF THEM DECIDED TO AVENGE HIM. THEY PURSUED AND KILLED THE ASSISTANT BEFORE THEY, TOO, WERE SENTENCED TO DEATH.

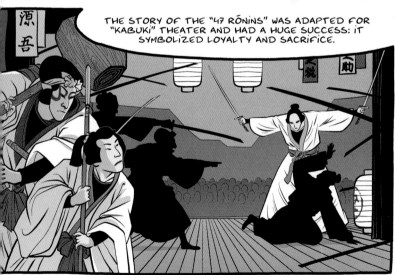

THE STORY OF THE "47 RONINS" WAS ADAPTED FOR "KABUKI" THEATER AND HAD A HUGE SUCCESS: IT SYMBOLIZED LOYALTY AND SACRIFICE.

DURING THIS ENTIRE PERIOD OF PEACE GOVERNED BY THE SHOGUNS, JAPAN CHOSE TO ISOLATE ITSELF FROM THE REST OF THE WORLD TO PRESERVE ITS TRADITIONAL SPIRIT, VIEWED AS AN IDEAL THAT THE SAMURAI EMBODIED.

IN 1633, THE SHOGUN IEMITSU TOKUGAWA FORBADE ALL CONTACT WITH STRANGERS.

IN THE 19TH CENTURY, EVERYTHING SUDDENLY CHANGED. EUROPEANS AND AMERICANS FORCED JAPAN TO OPEN UP TO TRADE.

SOME SAMURAI BLAMED THIS WEAKNESS ON THE SHOGUN. SO, THEY SUPPORTED EMPEROR MUTSUHITO WHEN HE REGAINED POWER IN 1867.

THE RETURN OF THE EMPEROR, HOWEVER, MARKED THE RETURN OF THE SAMURAI!

IT WAS THE BEGINNING OF THE "MEIJI" ERA, WHICH MODERNIZED JAPAN.

THE ARMY BECAME NATIONAL: ALL JAPANESE HAD TO BE PART OF IT, NOT JUST SAMURAI.

HARAKIRI WAS FORBIDDEN IN 1868; CARRYING A SWORD, IN 1876.

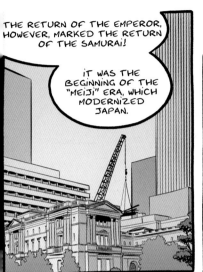

THESE DECISIONS CAUSED ABOUT 30,000 SAMURAI TO REVOLT. AN ARMY OF 300,000 MEN EQUIPPED WITH FIREARMS FOUGHT THEM. IN 1877, THE LAST SAMURAI WERE KILLED AT THE BATTLE OF SHIROYAMA.

IT WAS THE SAMURAI'S FINAL BATTLE.

SO, THE SAMURAI DISAPPEARED--BUT THEY WERE STILL REMEMBERED AND RESPECTED.

EVEN SAIGŌ TAKAMORI--THE "LAST SAMURAI," WHO LED THE REVOLT IN 1877--IS CONSIDERED A HERO; THERE'S A STATUE OF HIM IN TOKYO.

IN THE ARMY, SOLDIERS CONTINUED TO BEHAVE LIKE SAMURAI, WITH LOYALTY AND SACRIFICE.

IN 1912, GENERAL NOGI COMMITTED SEPPUKU: ALTHOUGH HE WON THE BATTLE HE HAD LED, HE FELT THERE HAD BEEN TOO MANY CASUALTIES!

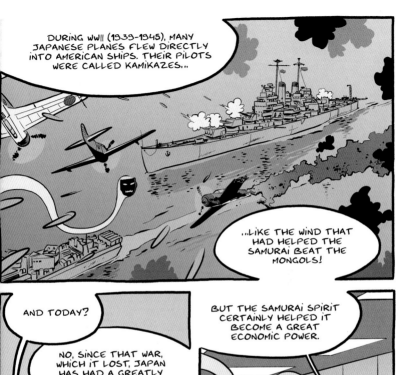

DURING WWII (1939-1945), MANY JAPANESE PLANES FLEW DIRECTLY INTO AMERICAN SHIPS. THEIR PILOTS WERE CALLED KAMIKAZES...

...LIKE THE WIND THAT HAD HELPED THE SAMURAI BEAT THE MONGOLS!

AND TODAY?

NO, SINCE THAT WAR, WHICH IT LOST, JAPAN HAS HAD A GREATLY REDUCED ARMY.

BUT THE SAMURAI SPIRIT CERTAINLY HELPED IT BECOME A GREAT ECONOMIC POWER.

EMPLOYEES ARE OFTEN REQUIRED TO BE "LOYAL" AND MAKE "SACRIFICES."

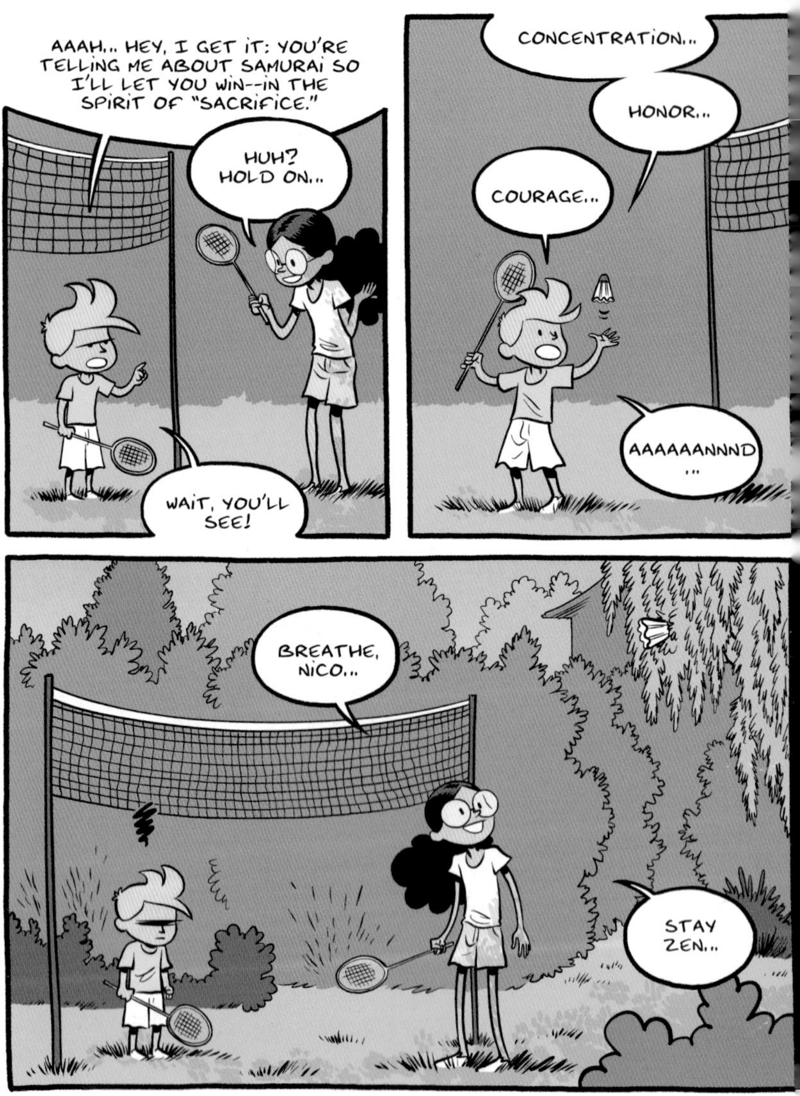
AAAH... HEY, I GET IT: YOU'RE TELLING ME ABOUT SAMURAI SO I'LL LET YOU WIN--IN THE SPIRIT OF "SACRIFICE."
HUH? HOLD ON...
WAIT, YOU'LL SEE!
CONCENTRATION...
HONOR...
COURAGE...
AAAAAANNND...
BREATHE, NICO...
STAY ZEN...

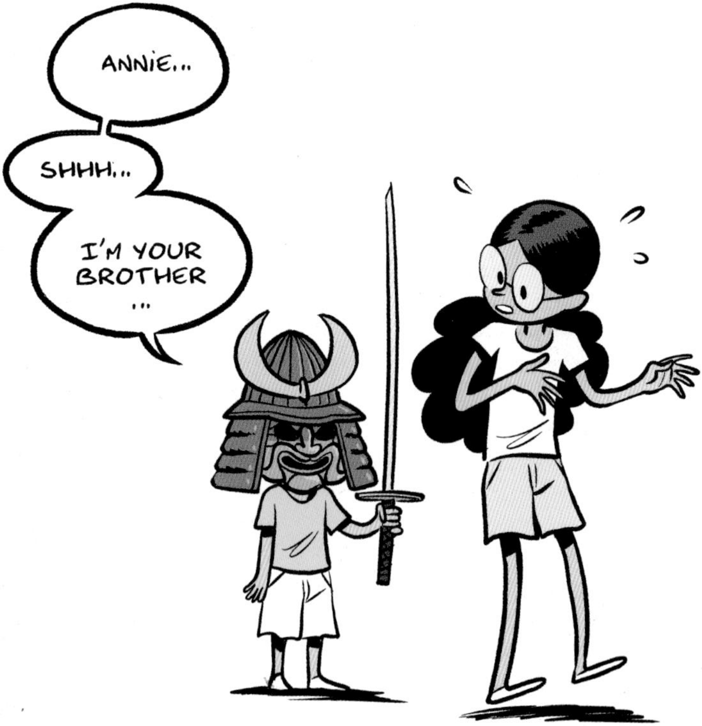
ANNIE...
SHHH...
I'M YOUR BROTHER
...

# Some People Who Made History

## Goro Nyudo Masamune
(1264-1343)

Considered one of the greatest blacksmiths of Japan, Masamune made a series of katanas of exceptional quality that could split a kabuto (helmet) in two. His swords, which bore his name, were passed on and wielded by legendary samurai such as Musashi. The "Honjo Masamune" katana belonged to the Tokugawa family of shoguns: all his heirs wore it until 1946, when it mysteriously disappeared.

## William Adams
(1564-1620)

The only European to become a samurai, Adams was a British navigator who went to Japan to trade in 1600. He was captured by the samurai of Tokugawa Ieyasu, whose trust he managed to win. When Tokugawa became shogun in 1603, Adams became his advisor and interpreter. Then he was made a samurai under the name of Miura Anjin. He married a Japanese woman and continued trading in Asia, never returning to England.

## Miyamoto Musashi
(1584-1645)

Skilled in combat at a very young age, Musashi fought his first duel when he was 13. At the age of 17, he took part in the great Battle of Sekigahara, where he was wounded. He then led the life of a wandering samurai and won some 60 duels, generally with a wooden sword. He is said to have beaten 60 members of a fencing school on his own. He fought—and won—his last duel in 1612 against Kojirō Sasaki, another famous samurai. He next devoted himself to teaching and then to writing and drawing.

## Nakano Takeko
(1847-1868)

Raised by a martial arts instructor, Nakano Takeko fought with the samurai in 1868 in the Battle of Aizu against the emperor's army. She fought with a warrior's naginata (lance with a blade). As she wasn't allowed to fight with men, she led a group of 20-30 women fighters nicknamed the "Women's Army." After being hit by a bullet, she asked her sister to cut off her head to avoid being captured by the enemy.

# Samurai and ninjas

Ninja means "stealthy person," but the name only came into use beginning around 1780. Before then, the term used was "shinobi," which meant the same thing.

A ninja was not an official fighter for a lord, like a samurai, but a warrior who hid: **he was tasked with spy missions and sabotage**, for example. Some- times defeated samurai or rōnin became ninjas.

Ninjas originally came from the southern moun- tainous regions of Japan, independent provinces that de- fended themselves during the 8th-9th centuries: they had no daimyos, and thus no samurai.

**The samurai, fighter in the light**

Ninjas weren't subject to bushido and undertook missions as assassinations, making them like **criminals**, which samurai honor could never accept.

**Ninjas were at risk long before samurai:** from 1579-1581, the daimyo Oda Nobunaga attacked the great ninja families of the south with his samurai. Many were slaughtered, but the survivors continued the tradition until the 19th century.

**Some shoguns employed ninjas:** this was the case with Tokugawa Ieyasu, who led Japan to peace in 1603. During the Edo period, samurai were used less because wars between the clans ceased, but ninjas were still used to protect the shogun or spy on opponents.

Samurai were taught "the paintbrush and the sword"; the ninja learned the techniques of "ninjutsu," which included hand-to-hand combat especially, but also **camouflage** and science (to manufacture poisons and explosives).

Like samurai, ninjas became **legendary characters in Japan** and throughout the entire world. They were viewed as powerful fighters.

The ninja,
shadow warrior

# The Daily Life of a Samurai

Samurai didn't wage war every day: during regular times, their lives were regulated by daily responsibilities.

## Morning

Samurai usually lived in a city in a closed district, separated from the rest of the population. They lived in a traditional wood home with movable interior walls made of paper.

At sunrise, a samurai meditated and got himself ready. He let his wife take care of the children and the home.

## Daytime

A samurai went to his daimyo's home early, protected him as he moved through the day, and did guard duty in the daimyo's castle or on his lands.

He ate a meal in the afternoon, followed by a bath in a warm spring to purify himself. After that, a samurai meditated in a Buddhist temple.

Daily training was necessary. If the samurai was an expert, he could be a combat instructor himself, teaching fighting techniques to the daimyo's other warriors.

After more guard duty, his day protecting the daimyo ended at sunset. The samurai, however, had to be available to the daimyo at all times, in case of any emergencies.

## Evening

To relax, samurai could go into town to drink sake, an alcoholic drink made from rice. They listened to music played by geishas, attended performances of Noh theater, or displayed their own dancing skills.

At bedtime, a samurai checked to make sure he had not acted in contradiction to his honor.

# Timeline

The shogun Minamoto no Yoritomo takes power in Japan—the beginning of samurai dominance.

The samurai prevent the Mongolian emperor Kublai Khan from invading Japan.

▼ 1192

▼ 1281

1603

1600

The start of the Edo period: Tokugawa Ieyasu becomes shogun and imposes peace. ▲

The Battle of Sekigahara, where roughly 200,000 samurai oppose each other. ▲

Around 1670

1703

The samurai Yamaga Sokō sets out the code of "bushido." ▲

47 rōnin commit seppuku after having avenged their executed master. ▲

Emperor Go-Daigo tries to retake power, but the shogun and his samurai eventually are victorious.

▼

**1331-1336**

The start of the Sengoku period of civil war, where the lords and their samurai oppose each other.

▼

**1467**

**1592-1598**

**1543**

▲

Japanese samurai fail to conquer Korea.

▲

Firearms are introduced in Japan by the Portuguese, which makes the samurai more vulnerable.

**1876**

**1877**

▲

The emperor forbids wearing a sword and reorganizes the Japanese army.

▲

After revolting, the samurai are crushed by the army.

# WATCH OUT FOR PAPERCUTZ

Welcome to the twelfth incredibly informative MAGICAL HISTORY TOUR graphic novel, this time exploring the world of "The Samurai," skillfully scripted by Fabrice Erre and stunningly illustrated by Sylvain Savoia and brought to you by Papercutz, those Zen-like folks dedicated to publishing great graphic novels for all ages. I'm Jim Salicrup, the Editor-in-Chief and The Ham on Wry punster, here with some behind-the-scenes Papercutz news…

*"Hello, I Must Be Going." –sung by Groucho Marx as Captain Spaulding in the 1930 film, Animal Crackers*

Well, it may no longer be news, more like very recent history, as it has already reported on Forbes.com that Papercutz has been purchased by Mad Cave Studios. The new Papercutz Editorial Director is Rex Ogle, who has worked at Marvel and DC Comics, as well as Scholastic and Little Brown for Young Readers. He's worked on everything from *LEGO* and *Minecraft* to *Star Wars* and *Buffy the Vampire Slayer*. When he's not editing books, he's either reading or writing them. Joining Rex

© 2004 by Simon & Schuster, Inc.

will be Senior Editor Zohra Ashpari, who was previously an editor at Tapas Media and has worked within the editorial departments of Scholastic and Tor Books. And completing the new editorial team will be Assistant Editor Stephanie Brooks, who started as an editorial intern at NBM before becoming my Assistant Managing Editor at Papercutz. Welcome, Rex, Zohra, and Stephanie! The future of Papercutz is certainly in good hands!

A bit more history… Over twenty years ago, graphic novel pioneer and NBM publisher, Terry Nantier, had the brilliant concept of starting yet another graphic novel publishing company— this one devoted to graphic novels for all ages. Terry asked me to be his partner and Editor-in-Chief in this crazy new venture, for which I readily agreed. I had started at Marvel Comics in 1972 when I was fifteen years old. 2022 marks my 50th anniversary of working in comics!

The first Papercutz comicbook, THE HARDY BOYS, was published in 2004, and in 2005, the first Papercutz graphic novels, THE HARDY BOYS and NANCY DREW saw print. And we've been at it ever since, through a world-wide Great Recession in 2008 and the recent global Covid Pandemic. But after almost twenty years Terry and I decided it was time for others to take Papercutz up to the next level, and that's where Mad Cave Studios comes in. While there was virtually no competition in the kids graphic novel category when we started, now almost every comics and book publisher is producing graphic novels for kids. Mad Cave Studios is better equipped to handle that kind of fierce competition.

For Terry and me, it's a little like Papercutz is one of our children that has grown up and is going off to college. While we both will still be around for a while as consultants to make the transition go as smoothly as possible, eventually we'll be moving on, leaving our baby in the very capable hands of Mad Cave Studios.

There are way too many people I'd like to thank for making my time at Papercutz over the years so wonderful. Terry, of course, the best publishing partner I could ever imagine! All of our writers, artists, letterers, colorists, production people, and of course, my invaluable, hard-working Managing Editors Michael Petranek, Bethany Bryan, Suzannah Rowntree, Jeff Whitman, and Stephanie Brooks. And of course, all of you, the Papercutz fans who have supported us over the years, with a special shout out to Rachel Boden, one of our biggest fans.

MAGICAL HISTORY TOUR will be back soon, in the 13th graphic novel, exploring "Marie Curie: A Life in Science." This will also be my final *Watch Out for Papercutz* column in MAGICAL HISTORY TOUR, but in light of the great news regarding Mad Cave Studios taking over, may my last words simply be, watch out for Papercutz—the best is yet to come!

## STAY IN TOUCH!

EMAIL: salicrup@papercutz.com
WEB: www.papercutz.com
TWITTER: @papercutzgn
INSTAGRAM: @papercutzgn
FACEBOOK: PAPERCUTZGRAPHICNOVELS
Go to papercutz.com and sign up for the free Papercutz e-newsletter!

Thanks,

**Fabrice Erre** has a Ph.D. in History and teaches Geography and History at the *Lycée Jean Jaures* near Montpellier, France. He has written a thesis on the satirical press, writes the blog *Une anne au lycée (A Year in High School)* on the website of *Le Monde*, one of France's top national newspapers, and has published several comics.

**Sylvain Savoia** draws the *Marzi* series, which tells the history of Poland as seen through the eyes of a child. He has also drawn *Les Esclaves oubliés de Tromelin (The Forgotten Slaves of Tromelin)*, which won the *Academie de Marine de Paris* prize.

# ORE GREAT GRAPHIC NOVEL SERIES AVAILABLE FROM PAPERCUTZ

**ASTERIX**

**ASTRO MOUSE AND LIGHT BULB**

**ATTACK OF THE STUFF**

**BRINA THE CAT**

**THE CASAGRANDES**

**CAT & CAT**

**THE FLY**

**FUZZY BASEBALL**

**GEEKY F@B 5**

**GERONIMO STILTON REPORTER**

**GILLBERT**

**LOLA'S SUPER CLUB**

**THE LOUD HOUSE**

**MELOWY**

**THE MYTHICS**

**THE NIGHTMARE BRIGADE**

**THE ONLY LIVING GIRL**

**SCHOOL FOR EXTRATERRESTRIAL GIRLS**

**THE SISTERS**

**THE SMURFS TALES**

# PAPERCUTZ
## WWW.PAPERCUTZ.COM
### ALSO AVAILABLE WHERE EBOOKS ARE SOLD.

# WHERE WILL THE MAGICAL HISTORY TOUR BRING ANNIE AND NICO NEXT?

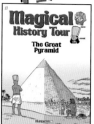

**The Great Pyramid**

**The Great Wall of China**

**Hidden Oil**

**The Crusades and the Holy Wars**

**The Plague History of a Pandemic**

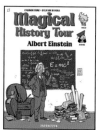

**Albert Einstein**

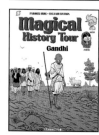

**Gandhi**

**Vikings**

**The Titanic Shipwreck of a Giant**

**The First Steps on the Moon**

**Slavery A Crime Against Humanity**

**The Samurai**

# Magical History Tour

Graphic novels are available wherever books are sold and at libraries everywhere.